PIERO VENTURA

MAN and the HORSE

G.P. Putnam's Sons   New York

Copyright © 1980 by Arnoldo Mondadori Editore S.p.A., Milano
English translation copyright © 1982
by Arnoldo Mondadori Editore S.p.A., Milano
All rights reserved. Published simultaneously in Canada by
General Publishing Co. Limited, Toronto.
Originally published in Italy by Arnoldo Mondadori Editore,
1980, under the title L'UOMO A CAVALLO
Printed and bound in Italy by Officine Grafiche di
Arnoldo Mondadori Editore, Verona
First Impression

Library of Congress Cataloging in Publication Data
Ventura, Piero.
Man and the horse.
Translation of L'uomo a cavallo.
Summary: Traces the history of man's association
with the horse from prehistoric times to the present.
1. Horses—History—Juvenile literature.
2. Animals and civilization—Juvenile literature.
[1. Horses—History.   2. Animals and civilization] I. Title.
SF283.V3813   909   82-386
ISBN 0-399-20842-9   AACR2

One day in the distant past, one of our ancestors sprang onto the back of a horse. From that moment, life changed for both man and horse, and a relationship that was complex and enduring was born.

As man entered the dawn of civilization, the beginning of our history, the horse was with him, helping him to change civilization—sometimes for the better and sometimes not. The horse was there to help plow, hunt, travel, migrate, explore, trade, and wage war. Without the horse, the path of history would have been different.

The Greeks immortalized the relationship between man and horse in their creation of the mythical centaur, who was half man and half horse. And according to the Bible, horse and man will be together to the last, for it is the Four Horsemen of the Apocalypse who will announce the end of the world.

A Cave Painting

In a cave in south-central France, more than fifteen thousand years ago, someone sketched beautiful images of horses on the walls. This remarkable painting is among the earliest-known drawings of horses.

But it would be centuries before we would domesticate and ride the horse. In primitive times, this wild creature—shy, suspicious, and extremely fast—was trapped and caught for food.

Reindeer Riders

We don't know exactly when or where people began to ride the horse, but we do know that the Mongolian people, forty centuries before Christ, migrated on reindeer. The spreading plains and the rich grazing lands of the steppes of north-central Asia, where they lived, were ideal terrain for wild horses. These reindeer riders were probably among the first to capture and ride horses for hunting and traveling from place to place.

An Assyrian Lion Hunt

Human beings were skilled riders long before writing appeared in our history. Archeological finds reveal that horses were used for hunting and for war. A major breakthrough appears in this representation of a relief found in the remains from Assyrian civilization—a two-wheeled chariot pulled by horses.

Here the king, Assurnasirpal, surrounded by warriors on horseback, hunts lions from a chariot using a bow and a javelin. With a driver to steer, Assurnasirpal was free to take aim and shoot accurately. Chariots quickly spread to the Mediterranean peoples such as the Egyptians.

A Chariot for the Pharaoh

Here the young Egyptian pharaoh Tutankhamen stands in his hunting chariot. By 1600 B.C., the Egyptians were using chariots for hunting, racing, and war. They made them lighter and more flexible than the Assyrian chariot because of the flat, sandy land of the Nile Valley.

The body was made of wood, covered with painted leather, and often decorated with metal applications. The light wooden wheels had six spokes and were reinforced with a rim of sewn leather.

War chariots, pulled by pairs of horses and manned by a driver and an archer, were the strength of the army. Egyptians never fought in the saddle; horsemen were used only as messengers and standard-bearers.

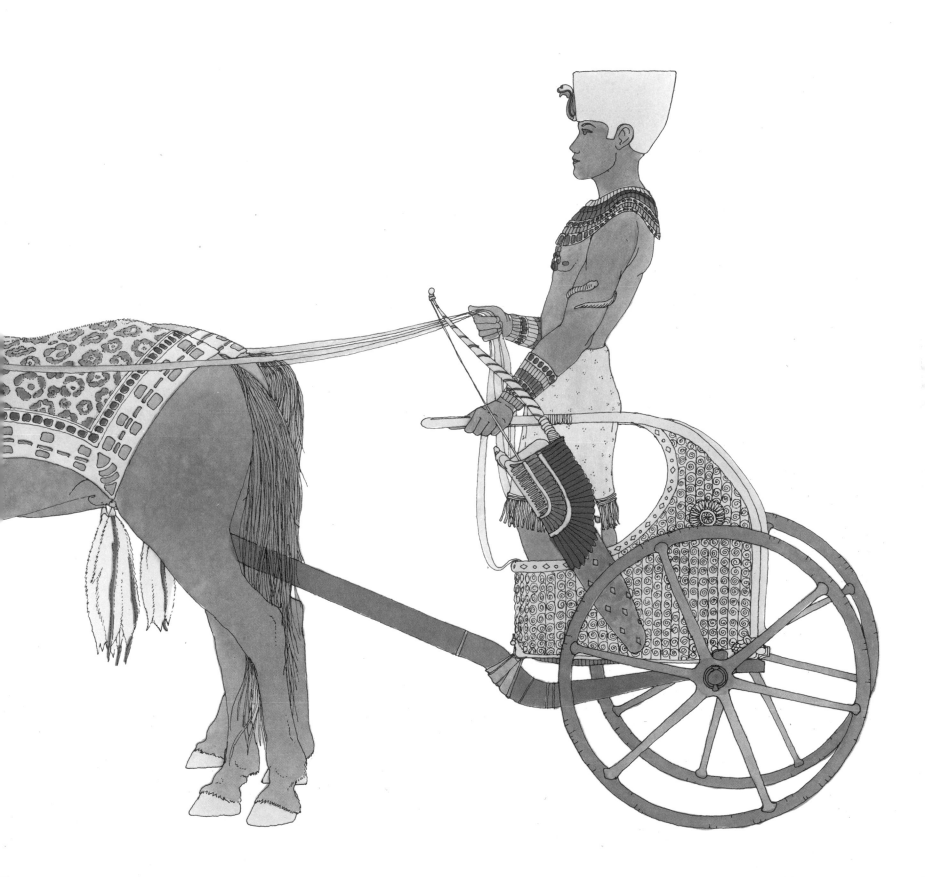

A Shield for the Roman Empire

Although war chariots were effective on the flatlands of Egypt, they were not practical in the hills of southern Italy, where the Roman army was growing in power.

The strength of the Roman legions were the infantrymen, with only a small cavalry. A foot soldier alone was no match for a warrior in a chariot, but when groups of soldiers arranged themselves in squares, protected by shields and holding sharp pikes, they were a strong opponent. Called a phalanx, this formation was adopted by the Roman legions and their might increased.

The cavalry played a larger part too. Men on horseback could explore more territory and patrol the hills while the legions advanced below. And they could effectively hinder the retreat of an enemy force.

A Roman Cavalry Officer

As the Roman army grew more powerful and marched on lands outside of Italy, the cavalry was more effective. It grew in size and was divided into two divisions, light and heavy.

This man is a decurion, the head of a heavy cavalry division. He wore iron-plated armor over a lorica, or covering, of light leather, and a helmet which protected his face. He was armed with a javelin and a long sword. The saddle was made of wood and leather with four pommels on the corners for supporting and gripping. Unlike saddles today, it had no stirrups.

The Romans were great horse breeders. They raised horses for war, parades, racing, and working.

In the Far East

In India and China, cavalry divisions were an important part of the army, and rich noblemen used them for hunting and traveling.

By 200 B.C., Chinese emperors had an effective postal service using horses, which played a significant role in their ability to control vast territories.

Here we see a Chinese emperor with his court taking a pleasure trip through the mountains of northern China. Soldiers ride ahead and behind the party. The emperor and his aides travel on horseback, while his wife and her ladies are carried in a two-wheeled cart covered with a pagoda-shaped roof.

With Feet in Stirrups

We don't know when stirrups were first used in Europe or who introduced them, but they changed the way soldiers rode and fought on horseback. A stirrup is a metal or leather ring which hangs down from a strap on either side of the saddle, and into which the rider places his or her feet.

It seems incredible that a simple development could have such an

impact, but in battle it meant that a soldier could rise up in the saddle and strike down with great force without losing his balance, or carry out a galloping attack with a lance in a fixed position.

Stirrups also made riding more comfortable and easier for both horse and rider. They allowed a soldier to wear heavier, more protective armor. Now the horseman had an even greater advantage over a man fighting on foot.

The Oath of the Sword

When the Barbarians—warring, nomadic tribes—invaded southern Europe in the fourth century, the power of the Roman Empire declined, and five hundred years of war, destruction, and hunger followed. Out of this came a new way of life called the feudal system.

Now the powerful person in a land was the lord, who owned large properties. He was owed allegiance by his knights, who fought for him, and by his peasants, who worked the land.

Here a lord looks down from the top of the castle steps where he receives the Oath of the Sword from his company of knights. This was a formal act of obedience and loyalty before battle and an important symbol of the bond that united the feudal lord to his knights.

The Green Flag of the Prophet

In a part of the world far from Europe, the Arabs lived, mostly as shepherds and nomads, in small rival tribes on the edge of the great southern deserts. They had little contact with Europe or the Mediterranean lands.

But with the birth of the prophet Muhammad in A.D. 570, a period followed in which the Arabs united as a strong, aggressive people, and attempted to conquer Europe. They ruled parts of Spain for many centuries.

Bound together by their Islamic faith and riding under the green flags embossed with a half-moon, they advanced and conquered on their remarkable Arabian horses. Fast, intelligent, and brave, these horses were the ancestors of our thoroughbred horses.

Although invaders and conquerors, the Arabs were also a creative, intelligent people who thrived as administrators wherever they went. They made great contributions in the fields of medicine, astronomy, architecture, and mathematics, and we still use their mathematical symbols, Arabic numerals.

The Splendor of Persia

Islam reached the peak of its development in the Middle East. Cities such as Baghdad, Damascus, and Aleppo grew into splendid, rich, bustling centers, ruled intelligently and wisely by men called caliphs.

Here we see a representation of hunters riding the legendary Nisaean horse, bred by Persian kings. It reflects the refined, prosperous life-style in the East, which contrasted greatly with the poor living conditions in Europe during the same period.

Trade Between East and West

For centuries a slow river of horsemen and camels traveling in single file traded between East and West. They carried silk, porcelain, and spices across burning deserts, over steep trails, and through snow-covered mountain valleys into Europe.

Much later, along these same trails and with the descendants of these same Mongolian drivers, the great Venetian traveler Marco Polo would reach China and the Kublai Khan toward the end of the thirteenth century.

A Medieval Knight

This is the way a feudal knight looked in the eleventh century. Covered from head to foot in chain mail with a helmet to protect his face and head, he carried an oval shield made of iron covered in wood, a sword, an ax, and a dagger. But his most deadly weapon was a long wooden lance with an iron tip.

Large horses were bred to carry his great weight; still, every knight had to use several horses during one campaign. Lighter horses were used for moving from one place to another.

All of the horses, the equipment, and the persons whom knights needed to take care of them were funded by a feudal lord who turned over a piece of his land along with some of his peasants to the knight in return for his loyalty and services in battle. In this way a lord could raise his own army of knights when he needed them.

The Feudal Castle

This is a knight's castle, where his men practiced for battle while his peasants took care of the castle and worked his lands. The castle was built with strong, high walls surrounded by a moat so that it could be defended, even by a handful of people, from passing armies or unfriendly neighbors.

As the feudal way of life spread, lords and knights became more powerful and cities started to decline. Peasants and craftsmen began to gather around the castles, creating a feudal hamlet or village.

Harnessing the Horse

Although most people still farmed, more and more of them worked as craftsmen, making and improving tools and inventing new means of making labor easier and more productive. One of the most simple yet revolutionary discoveries was a better way of harnessing a horse. Until then, a horse was tied to its load with straps around its neck. This placed

a severe strain on the horse and it could not pull a load comfortably or effectively. By putting a large, padded collar lower down on the horse's shoulders, the weight it could carry was doubled.

Now it was possible to plow the fields deeper and produce larger harvests. With more food available for everyone, population increased and more people could work at other things such as crafts or commerce.

Knights for Hire

Eventually, all of Europe except the Scandinavian countries adopted the feudal way of life. But as the population became larger, not every knight or lord's son could have his own castle and property. Gradually, those knights who had no land of their own banded together into groups called "lances" and hired themselves out for money. While songs and stories have idealized knights who went on quests and crusades, these lances of knights were mercenary soldiers whose trade was war. Now kings or princes could hire large numbers of armed men to fight for them if they could pay their wages.

Arms and Armor

Toward the end of the thirteenth century, plated armor replaced chain mail. The craftsmen who made the armor had to produce better-quality steel and fashion it into a design that let the knight move and fight freely.

The man on the right wears Gothic armor made in Nuremberg and the one on the left wears a Milanese design. As the designs got more complicated, armor became more expensive.

Chivalry in Crisis

When farming was the main occupation of the people, the feudal lord of the castle held the power and prestige, and land was more important than money. But as soldiers for hire became more and more expensive, money became increasingly important. As trade and commerce developed, living conditions improved, and cities blossomed as centers of crafts and commerce.

Expensive armor, skill in the art of war, and knighthood were no longer enough to maintain power and control. Early in the fourteenth

century, the people of Courtrai, in Flanders, armed only with pikes, sticks, and farming tools, stood up against a company of knights. Then an even more important event took place during the Hundred Years' War between the English and the French. Armed with their longbows, English archers fought and defeated the supposedly superior French knights at Crécy, France.

But the final blow to knighthood and the feudal system came with firearms. This man holds a harquebus, a gun fired from a support.

Jousts and Tourneys

Toward the end of the fifteenth century, the kings of Spain, France, England, and Portugal grew more powerful. Now a king with a nation of people who served in the army or worked and paid taxes to support his army replaced the feudal system.

The castle as a seat of power began to disappear, although its traditions continued. Noblemen still wore their armor as symbols of prestige and power, but infantrymen were the strength of the king's army.

Armor had grown so heavy and grotesque that it was useless in battle, but it was perfect for the sport of jousting, at which the knights of the period excelled. Two contestants faced each other on horseback, wearing armor and carrying a lance. With a palisade, or wooden barrier, between them, they raced at each other, attempting to break their lance by striking their opponent. A broken lance showed that the contestant had struck his target, and he was proclaimed the victor.

Discovering the New World

In 1492, Christopher Columbus, sailing under orders of the King of Spain, set out to reach the Indies by sailing west across the Atlantic Ocean. He landed on the island of San Salvador in the Bahamas. Columbus didn't know it, but he had discovered the New World and opened up fresh territory for exploration from Europe.

Then, early in the sixteenth century, a Spaniard, Hernando Cortes, arrived on the shores of Mexico with a few hundred men, sixteen horses, and several cannon. The land was ruled by the Aztec Indians, a highly complex, advanced society. Yet, in only a few years, the Aztecs would collapse in the face of internal problems and the Spanish invaders.

The inhabitants of North America had never seen a horse, but the rich grazing land and lots of fresh water made it an ideal place for horses. As the Spanish brought over more horses, some escaped or were abandoned. They gave birth to foals, and by the seventeenth century, bands of wild horses had begun to grow and spread.

Muskets and Musketeers

In Europe, during the seventeenth century, the armies of the kings were growing larger as more men joined to earn a living as professional soldiers. Armies consisted largely of infantrymen, although a brief attempt was made to build the cavalry. But it wasn't practical in the face of the field artillery and firearms, which dominated the battles. Still, the horse remained a symbol of prestige for officers and commanders. Armor was replaced by splendid, colorful uniforms like the one worn here by a French musketeer. The knight's heavy sword was abandoned for a slender rapier, a light sword with a cup-shaped handgrip. The musketeer also carried a short saddle pistol which was neither accurate nor powerful.

The Hussars

"The greatest secret in the carrying out of a war and the masterpiece of a good general lies in starving the enemy. Hunger weakens the enemy much more surely than the bravery of others, with fewer risks and less danger than by fighting." These words by Frederick the Great of Prussia perfectly capture the cynical spirit of the endless destructive wars of the eighteenth century.

While the soldiers' role was to lay siege to fortified cities in an attempt to starve them into surrendering, a new and not so honorable use was found for the cavalry.

Irregular units called hussars were organized to plunder and pillage the countryside. Dressed in special uniforms that distinguished them from the regular troops, the hussars attacked and robbed the civilian population, and, as often happens in war, the ordinary people suffered the most.

The Samurai

In Japan, a feudal way of life similar to that of Europe produced horsemen called samurai.

The samurai were those sons of feudal landowners who were not the firstborn and therefore could not inherit land, so they went into the service of other feudal lords as warriors. A strict code of conduct was developed for the samurai. Unlike European knights, they never became landowners or attained the rank of nobleman.

The samurai took part in the long wars of medieval Japan, but the eventual appearance of firearms never deterred them as it had the knights of Europe. What brought about their decline was the long period of peace that came when the seventeenth-century dynasty of the Tokugawa united the country.

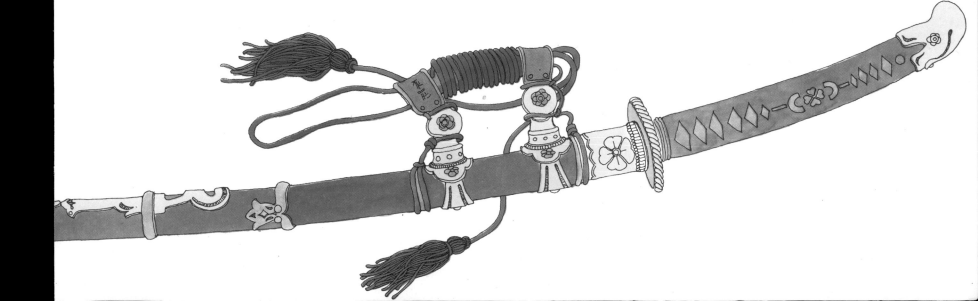

The Cavalry Charge

Once again, for about a hundred years, the cavalry came back into use in European armies. At the command of "Charge!" the cavalry, arranged in closed ranks and armed with sabers and lances, hurled itself full gallop at the enemy lines. Men and horses went down by the hundreds in the face of artillery and small-arms fire from a thin line of infantry. But those riders who did get through the lines created confusion and scattered the infantry as they wielded their terrible curved sabers. It was another brutal way of waging war.

The Ravages of War

Here is a scene of devastation on the snow-covered plains of Russia, where the imperial dream of the emperor Napoleon ended in the early nineteenth century. Battered by fierce snow and sleet and cut off from supply lines, his armies floundered and died.

During the nineteenth century the cavalry was once again a small elite part of an army, sporting officers wearing splendid uniforms and carrying

colorful pennants. Large military farms bred horses best suited to the various regiments such as the Dragoons, Lancers, Hunters, and Guides. Proud officers competed with one another, showing off their handsome horses along the streets of garrison towns.

But in spite of the fanfare and splendor, the reality of war represented here could be seen on battlefields around the world.

The Stagecoach

The horse was an important part of the economy in peacetime. With the spread of steam-powered machines and the growth of factories, countries were clearly headed for an industrial revolution.

Millions of people needed to travel, and thousands of coaches, like this one in England, carried people and baggage from one postal station to another. It was the start of mass transportation and would lead to the steam train and eventually to the automobile.

Buffalo Hunting

Before the Spaniards brought horses to North America, native American
Indians lived on the vast prairie lands as food gatherers and farmers. But
as herds of horses spread across the land, the Indians learned to use
them, and eighteenth-century European explorers described the Plains
Indians as skillful horsemen.

   Horses allowed the Indians to follow the great herds of migrating
buffalo and hunt them for meat and skins. Here is a typical Plains Indian
camp. The cone-shaped tents were made out of buffalo skin, and one can
see some of the Indians riding in from hunting while others work on the
skins or hang them on racks to dry.

Scout and Officer

As more Europeans emigrated to America, more people began moving west to make a new life. The white settlers wanted to make homes on their own land, but the native American Indians' way of living did not include owning land. They roamed freely, hunting and fishing, and these

conflicting ideas started problems
between the white settlers and the
Indians.

The U.S. Army Cavalry, whose job
it was to protect the settlers and keep
law and order, was a part of the
conflict. Here is a cavalry officer in his
blue uniform opposite a scout who
knew the Western lands well and
could guide the cavalry.

Frontier Towns

As more people moved west, frontier towns sprang up along the trails that led across the continent. Made of wooden buildings constructed almost overnight, these towns provided hotels, banks, stores, shops, and restaurants for anyone passing through and for the farmers and ranchers who lived on the surrounding lands.

The towns had doctors, dentists, blacksmiths, veterinarians, and saddlemakers, but perhaps best remembered are the cowboys, who came to symbolize the American West.

The Cowboy and His Horse

A famous American writer once described cowboys as "the only human beings with four hoofs." The cowboy's most treasured possessions were his horse and his saddle, and with them he made his living.

In 1790, just under four million people lived in America. Just one hundred years later, this number had leaped to sixty-three million and the stream of immigrants kept coming. All of these people had to eat, and the cowboys were the backbone of the cattle industry, which supplied meat for the whole country.

In the fall and winter months, the cowboy lived on the ranch and looked after the grazing herds. He had a warm bed to sleep in, hot food to eat, and time off. But in the spring and summer, his work was hard and constant. With other cowboys, he drove the cattle to market, making journeys that lasted anywhere from a few weeks to a few months. Keeping the herd moving and under control, and often crossing difficult terrain or battling bad weather and fierce storms, made a cowboy's job difficult and dangerous.

Carriages and Coaches

Even though the power of steam and
electricity was used more and more, in the
nineteenth century people still traveled by
coach, and the horse remained an
important part of everyday life.

Large strong wagons and different types
of coaches and carriages were designed for

various uses: transporting goods and people, maneuvering in city traffic, carrying supplies in wartime or for work in factories or on farms.

Words such as axle, hub, mudguard, brake, and hood, which we connect with cars, all come from the names of coach and carriage parts.

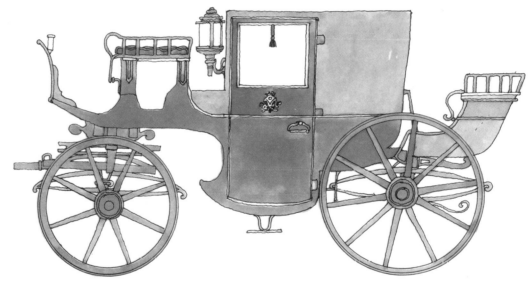

Traffic and Transportation

Terrible traffic and noise are not products of twentieth-century living. A few years before the birth of Christ, to cut down on traffic congestion in Rome, the emperor Augustus ordered that wagons carrying merchandise travel on the streets of the city only at night. Imagine the noise for all those million people trying to sleep.

An eighteenth-century coachman complained about the traffic accidents in the streets of Paris.

And in the second half of the nineteenth century, London, New York, and Paris all had severe traffic problems. One of London's solutions was to build the first underground railroad in 1863.

Although trains and ships carried baggage and people over long distances, horses were still used for shorter travel and in the cities. In fact, the horse population reached its highest at the end of the nineteenth century, with over one hundred twenty million horses at work around the world.

A typical horse-drawn vehicle of the day was this tram in Manchester, England. A carriage that could hold between thirty and forty people was pulled along a track by a team of two or four horses.

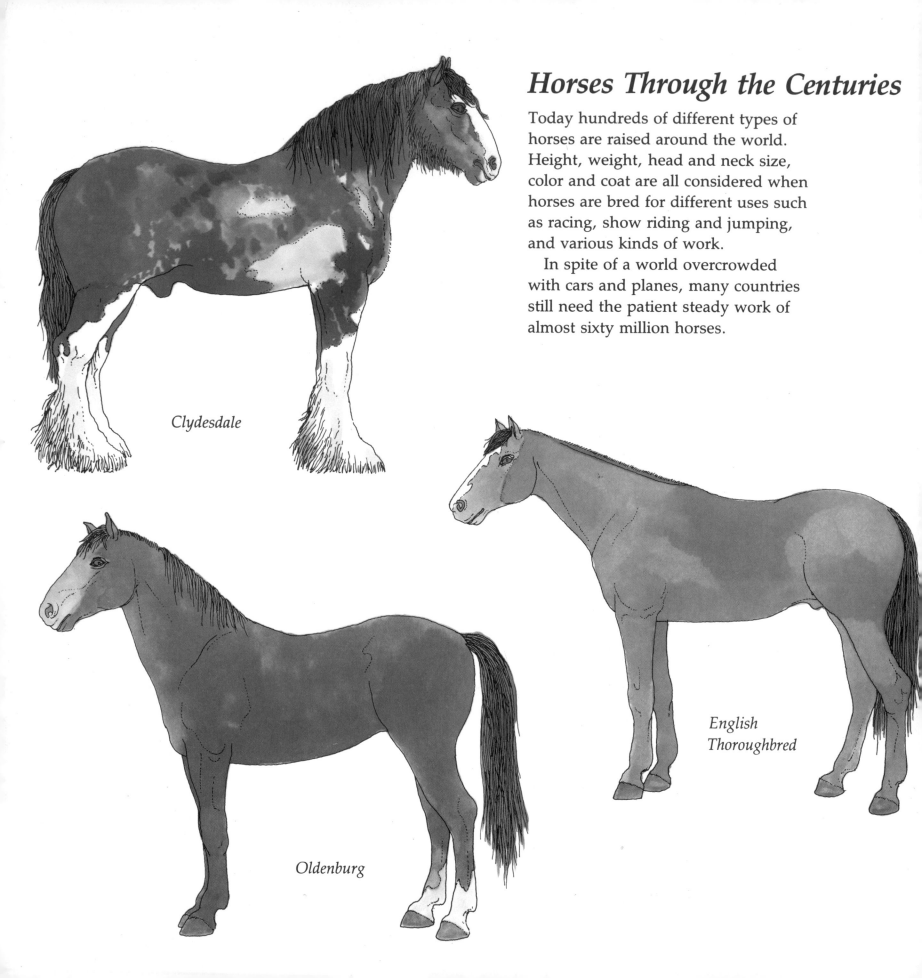

Horses Through the Centuries

Today hundreds of different types of horses are raised around the world. Height, weight, head and neck size, color and coat are all considered when horses are bred for different uses such as racing, show riding and jumping, and various kinds of work.

In spite of a world overcrowded with cars and planes, many countries still need the patient steady work of almost sixty million horses.

Clydesdale

English Thoroughbred

Oldenburg

Hanoverian

Jutland

Friesian

Lippizaner

Andalusian

Arabian

Fjord

Akhal-Teke

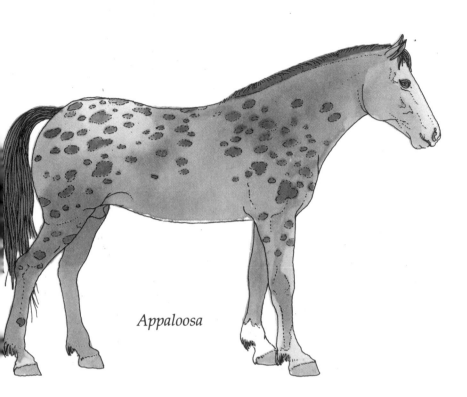

Appaloosa

Noriker

Palomino

In America

All over America today, horses can be seen at work on small farms, grazing peacefully in grassy meadows, executing complicated maneuvers in a show ring, or sailing high over a stone wall in a jumping competition. And what is more beautiful than the thoroughbreds that grace tracks around the country, where horses such as Secretariat excite the imagination of everyone?

But America has a wild-horse legacy which must not be forgotten. The mustang, descendant of the Spanish horses, still survives in remote, rugged areas of the West. That sturdy, tough little horse which remains wild and free in the face of adversity stands as a reminder of the importance of freedom, independence, and survival.